Core Math Skills
Operations and Algebraic Thinking

# At the Carnival

**Understand and Apply Properties of Operations**

Ed Swazinski

**PowerKiDS** press ™

NEW YORK

Published in 2014 by The Rosen Publishing Group, Inc.
29 East 21st Street, New York, NY 10010

Book Design: Mickey Harmon

Photo Credits: Cover littleny/Shutterstock.com; p. 5 Photos.com/Thinkstock.com; p. 7 Lisa F. Young/Shutterstock.com; p. 9 sam100/Shutterstock.com; p. 11 meirion matthias/Shutterstock.com; p. 13 Mircea BEZERGHEANU/Shutterstock.com; p. 15 June Marie Sobrito/Shutterstock.com; p. 17 Erik E. Cardona/Shutterstock.com; p. 19 Martin Anderson/Shutterstock.com; p. 21 Stephen Bonk/Shutterstock.com; p. 22 Mike Flippo/Shutterstock.com.

Swazinski, Ed.
At the carnival: understand and apply properties of operations / Ed Swazinski.
  p. cm. – (Core math skills. Operations and algebraic thinking)
Includes index.
ISBN 978-1-4777-2058-5 (pbk.)
ISBN 978-1-4777-2059-2 (6-pack)
ISBN 978-1-4777-2210-7 (library binding)
1. Addition–Juvenile literature. 2. Subtraction–Juvenile literature. 3. Carnival. I. Title.
QA115.S92 2014
513.2'12–dc23

Manufactured in the United States of America

CPSIA Compliance Information: Batch #CS13RC: For further information contact Rosen Publishing, New York, New York at 1-800-237-9932.

Word Count: 284

# Contents

## The Best Part of Summer

Liam loves summer. A big **carnival** comes to town every year. There are so many things to see and do!

## Clowning Around

Liam sees a clown named Benny. He has 3 red balloons in one hand and 4 blue balloons in the other. He has 7 balloons in all!

$$3 + 4 = 7$$

Liam sees another clown named Bubbles. He has 4 red balloons and 3 blue balloons. Both clowns have 7 balloons.

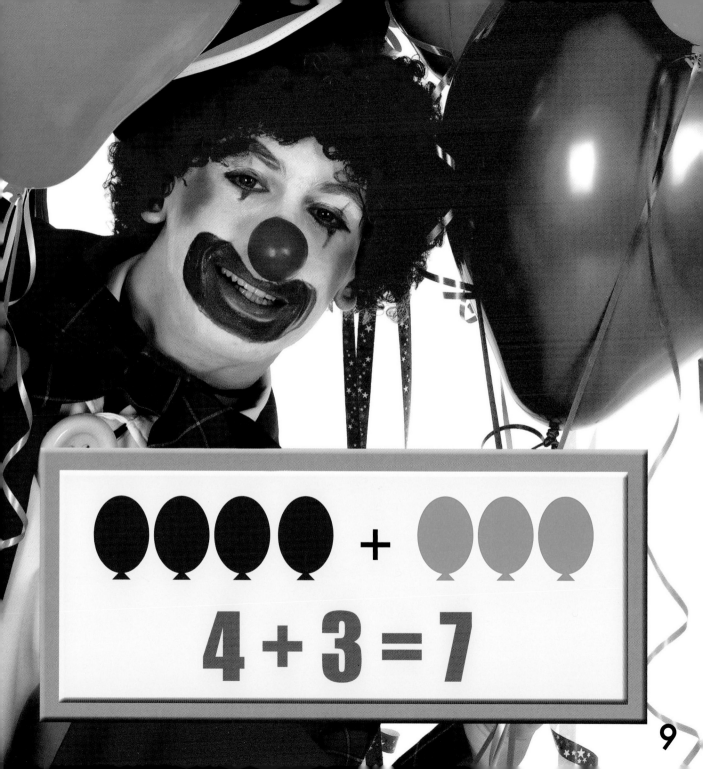

## Fun at the Petting Zoo

Next, Liam goes to the petting zoo. There are 3 sheep and 2 goats in one barn. There are 5 animals to pet!

3 + 2 = 5

There are 2 sheep and 3 goats in another barn. Liam can pet 5 animals here, too. He likes to pet the goats the most!

2 + 3 = 5

## Buying Cotton Candy

Liam wants to buy **cotton candy**. There are 3 bags of blue cotton candy, 4 bags of pink cotton candy, and 2 bags of yellow cotton candy. There are 9 bags in all.

$$3 + 4 + 2 = 9$$

15

Liam buys 3 bags of blue cotton candy and 2 bags of yellow cotton candy. That's 5 bags! He also buys 4 bags of pink cotton candy for his sister. How many bags does Liam buy altogether?

## Waiting for the Carousel

The best part of the carnival is the **carousel**.

6 people are waiting for the ride. 3 people get on it after the first turn. 2 people get on it after the next turn. 1 person is left in line.

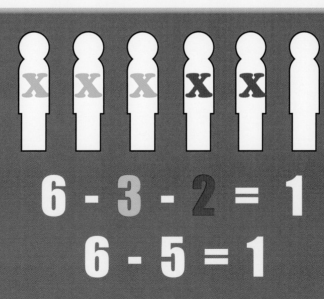

6 - 3 - 2 = 1

6 - 5 = 1

19

## Playing Games

Liam buys tickets to play 8 games. He plays 4 games of basketball and 2 games of bowling. He plays 6 games altogether. How many more games can he play?

8 - 4 - 2 = ?

8 - 6 = ?

21

Liam had fun at the carnival. He gives his last 2 tickets to his sister. She wins a prize at the duck pond! Everyone goes home with a smile.

# Glossary

**carnival** (KAHR-nuh-vuhl)  A fair that travels from place to place and has rides, games, and shows.

**carousel** (KEHR-uh-sehl)  A merry-go-round.

**cotton candy** (KAH-tuhn KAN-dee)  Fluffy sugar candy.

# Index

Due to the changing nature of Internet links, The Rosen Publishing Group, Inc., has developed an online list of websites related to the subject of this book. This site is updated regularly. Please use this link to access the list: www.powerkidslinks.com/cms/oat/atc